779•0924 Danly, Susan.
DAN
      Edward Weston in
      Los Angeles

$10.00

DATE			

Local

EDWARD WESTON IN LOS ANGELES

EDWARD WESTON IN LOS ANGELES

Frontispiece:
Self-portrait, 1909/10
Private collection.

Susan Danly and Weston J. Naef

A Catalogue for Exhibitions at

The Huntington Library

November 25, 1986–March 29, 1987

and

The J. Paul Getty Museum

November 25, 1986–February 1, 1987

Library of Congress No. 86-27083
ISBN 0-87328-092-x
© Copyright 1986
The Huntington Library and Art Gallery
San Marino, California

TABLE OF CONTENTS

The centennial of Edward Weston's birth on March 25, 1986 inspired much activity by museums, scholars, and collectors with regard to his art and life. More particularly it served to focus attention on his years in Los Angeles, the location of two distinct phases in his career. The earliest, from 1906 to 1923, saw him build an international reputation for his portraits and figure studies. The second, in the late 1930s, was also an especially productive period, when almost all of his photographs were made in the field. A Guggenheim grant in 1937–38 unchained him from the responsibility of maintaining a portrait practice and afforded him the freedom and financial support to undertake a large series of landscape photographs. This second Los Angeles phase culminated in the publication of his book, *California and the West,* in 1940.

The Los Angeles artistic and literary community has long maintained an interest in Weston's work, a fact accounting for the richness of Weston holdings in Southern California. The photographs illustrated here in full-page plates are representative of the Weston works in the Getty and Huntington collections and are included in the counterpart exhibitions at the respective institutions. The following catalogue essays discuss these works in relationship to Weston's contemporaries and within the context of his own stylistic development and life.

In researching and preparing the exhibitions for the Huntington Library and the J. Paul Getty Museum, we have received the advice and support of many people. We would like to thank Cole Weston, Mr. and Mrs. Leonard Vernon, who have opened their collections for research and lent to the Getty Museum's exhibition, and Jacob Zeitlin who has shared his recollections of Weston and their mutual friends. Several institutions, particularly the Center for Creative Photography in Tucson, The Oakland Museum, The San Francisco Museum of Modern Art, Friends of Photography in Carmel, and The California Museum of Photography in Riverside, have been most helpful in providing access to Weston's photographs and archives. The Museum of Modern Art, The Metropolitan Museum, The Smithsonian Institution, The International Museum of Photography at George Eastman House, and Scripps College also provided illustrations for the essays in this volume.

Individual scholars have generously shared their thoughts on Weston's work and contributed greatly to our knowledge of his career. Professor Amy Conger and Naomi Sawelson-Gorse of the University of California at Riverside; Ben Maddow, Los Angeles; Amy Stark, Lawrence Fong, and Terence Pitts at the Center for Creative Photography; and James Alinder at the Friends of Photography have been especially supportive throughout this project. Stephen L. Schlesinger, the current Secretary of the John Simon Guggenheim Memorial Foundation, searched their records for Weston-Huntington correspondence and provided information on other Guggenheim photography grant recipients. Charis Wilson, in addition to spending a great deal of time discussing Weston's photographs with the staff of the Rare Books Department at the Huntington Library, also made available the original notes which she wrote while traveling with Weston during his Guggenheim grant years.

Finally, we wish to acknowledge the assistance of the following individuals who helped in the preparation of this catalogue and the exhibition at the Huntington Library: Brita Mack and Alan Jutzi in the Rare Book Department; Carol Verheyen and Jacqueline Dugas in the Art Division; and Guilland Sutherland in the Publications Department. Similarly, we owe a special thanks to the staff of the J. Paul Getty Museum, especially: Bret Waller, Associate Director for Education and Public Affairs; Andrea P.A. Belloli, Publications Department; Deborah Gribbon, Assistant Director for Curatorial Affairs; Joan Gallant, Victoria Blasco, Ernie Mack, and James Evans of the Department of Photographs; Leila York who typed the manuscript; and Robert Aitchison and Jim Hsieh who helped prepare photographs for exhibition.

Edward Weston arrived in Los Angeles on May 29, 1906, wearing a felt hat and flannel trousers and with his belongings packed in a little trunk, planning on a two-month visit that lasted for thirty years. In this inconspicuous way Weston's relationship began with the city of Los Angeles, a relationship as stormy as any of the human ones that are the substance of his popular biography. He migrated to Los Angeles from Chicago to be near his sister, May, who had cared for him after their mother's death when he was five years old and she fourteen. The influence of May on Edward Weston's life was profound; their father described it in a family scrapbook: "A mother could not have cared for a child more faithfully than she did; and they grew up with a double love, that of mother and son, and sister and brother."[1]

1 Untitled scrapbook begun by Edward Burbank Weston about 1910, 10. Edward Weston Archives. Center for Creative Photography, University of Arizona.

Edward Weston's artistic life seems to have been linked to an uncommon degree with his emotional and personal life. We know this because he saved the details of his own mature biography in letters and a journal he began to keep around 1915, the approximate time he was introduced to modern art. The journal entries dating from its commencement to 1923 were destroyed; the surviving journal entries, which date from the mid-1920s to the mid-1930s, have been edited and published by Nancy Newhall;[2] Weston's early letters have been researched and published by Ben Maddow,[3] who compiled them into the most detailed published biography of the artist. We are anxiously awaiting publication of Amy Conger's catalogue raisonné of Edward Weston's photographs,[4] and of her biography of his life through 1927 that is nearing completion. Weston was both a fluent writer for publication,[5] and himself a subject for other writers,[6] so that his own writings and those of others are important sources of information about his artistic life during the teens.

3 Ben Maddow, *Edward Weston: Fifty Years* (Millerton, 1978), 36.

5 Peter C. Bunnell, editor, *Edward Weston on Photography* (Salt Lake City, 1986).

6 Beaumont Newhall and Amy Conger, *Edward Weston Omnibus* (Salt Lake City, 1983).

7 See note 1 above.

2 Nancy Newhall, *The Daybooks of Edward Weston, Volume 1 Mexico* (Rochester, 1961) (hereafter cited as *Daybooks I*).

4 Amy Conger, "Edward Weston's Early Photography, 1903-1926," Ph.D dissertation, University of New Mexico, Albuquerque, 1982. I wish to thank Amy Conger for generously sharing information useful to writing this essay, and for her thoughtful reading of the text.

There is a considerable gap in our information about Weston's biography between the boyhood period, covered by his father's recollections,[7] and 1923, when Weston's own *Daybooks* commence, after which there are a plentiful number of surviving letters. The enormous amount of information that exists about Weston's life in the 1920s and 1930s only serves to draw attention to the destruction of the earlier journal, and the element of mystery induced by that loss of textual evidence. There are, however, clues in unexpected places about Weston's life at the time, including his own photographs of 1915–1920.[8]

8 The autobiographical elements of Weston's photographs are discussed in Kathy Kelsey Foley, *Edward Weston's Gifts to his Sister* (Dayton Art Institute, 1978).

Photography may be a more inherently autobiographical art than other forms of picture-making because photographs are so deeply rooted in time and place. Edward Weston's photographs have yet to be studied for their autobiographical elements, an aspect that is particularly important in his earliest work. He made many more photographs between 1906 and 1915 than have survived. Those that have were saved through the efforts of the artist's

Plate 1.
Bathers, 1919
The J. Paul Getty Museum.

Fig. 1.
Art Institute of Chicago, 1906
Private collection.

Fig. 2.
Indian Woman, 1906
Private collection.

Fig. 3.
*San Pedro, Los Angeles, and
Salt Lake Railroad* (detail),
1906/1907
Private collection.

*With the exception of
Figs. 8 and 13, items
1-20 are attributed to
Edward Weston based
on stylistic and
circumstantial evidence.*

first wife, Flora Chandler, who was the mother of his four sons (Chandler, Neil, Brett, and Cole) and who compiled photographs he gave her into albums intended as family history.[9]

Let us look at some of these early Weston photographs for clues as to what they may reveal about his personality and the emergence of his artistic sensibility. One of the last things Weston did when he left Chicago on his way West was to take a photograph of the Art Institute of Chicago from the corner of Michigan and Monroe avenues [Fig. 1]. Weston's photograph of the Art Institute is as inauspicious as his arrival in Los Angeles, nothing more than a snapshot. However, it does raise the question of why he made it. Does it express the memory of many happy hours spent in the museum, or a longing to better understand its contents, or simply an admiration of the structure itself? We shall never know for sure. What we do know is that Weston spent the next decade searching for the definition of art itself.

Most of the photographs Weston made en route to Los Angeles are possibly more notable for the signature he scratched into the negatives than for their technique or compositions. The way he formed the "W" with curliques shows that he was still an adolescent at heart. The fact that he signed these photographs at all indicates the unconscious ambition to address an audience. They signal his confidence that he could guide us with his camera, using it metaphorically to point out what we might not observe of our own accord. One of these series is marked with an element of the genius that later brought him fame. The photograph of an Indian woman caught in the shadow of a railroad car [Fig. 2] reveals its subject through suggestion rather than declaration and is more than a record of this particular instant in time. In another study of the same women we see a face on which is etched the traces of a life lived in poverty and exposure to the natural elements. In these images Weston began to explore a theme that was to obsess him as a mature photographer: the nature of womanhood.

Weston arrived in California a month after the San Francisco earthquake and fire, full of idealism and very naive about the impact that geographical, social, intellectual, and aesthetic forces would have upon him. Although by 1906 he had become an advanced amateur photographer, it did not occur to him that photography could be either a fine art or a profession until he worked briefly at other occupations. His brother-in-law, John Seaman, got him on the payroll of the San Pedro, Los Angeles, & Salt Lake Railroad, a job that suited his outdoors spirit but for which he was temperamentally unsuited. A photograph from this period allows us to draw some conclusions about Weston's self-image at the age of twenty [Fig. 3]. He is dressed nattily in high-topped boots and riding breeches, an outfit that his imperious and outdoors-minded father may have presented to him as part of a wardrobe for

9 On loan to the Getty Museum are several albums compiled by Flora Weston: three bearing inscriptions respectively to Edward Chandler, Theodore Brett, and Cole Weston; two albums pertaining to the courtship of Edward and Flora; and one miscellaneous album containing photographs by Weston during his Mojonier studio period.

Fig. 4.
Flora Weston, 1909
Private collection.

the rugged West. His companions are dressed more practically in flannel shirts, denims, and ordinary engineer's boots. Weston may have seemed overprivileged and out of place on a survey crew.

It was Weston's sister May who introduced her brother to Flora Chandler, her closest friend. Flora, a woman six years his senior, soon became a favorite subject. The theme of womanhood cropped up again as Weston explored Flora's face [Fig. 4] and physique as though woman was an unknown and unknowable phenomenon. This photograph of Flora, reclining on her back with her arms raised seductively above her head, signals his growing mastery of the art of photography and marks the first evidence of sexuality as an important underlying theme in his work. The nude studies[10] of Margrethe Mather and Tina Modotti of almost fifteen years later, and those of Charis Wilson, Weston's second wife, of almost thirty years later have their first seed in this image.

Weston and Flora became engaged in 1907 or 1908. At first Weston was very eager to please her and her family, which was headed by Albion Chandler, a real-estate investor who had helped found the incorporated town of Tropico (today part of Glendale) in 1887.[11] It was surely to reassure the Chandlers that he had a means of supporting Flora that Weston returned to Chicago unexpectedly in late 1907 or early 1908 and enrolled at the Illinois College of Photography. Trade schools typically taught specialized photographic skills of various kinds such as how to use the newly invented electric flood and spot lights as well as efficient laboratory procedures. Indoor photography was stressed and lessons were aimed at imparting the skills needed to work in the kind of professional portrait studios that thrived in almost every town of any size. Weston learned the tried and true methods of creating photographs that would satisfy the customer and changed from earnest amateur to skillful professional.

This strategy paid off in the short run and he decided to turn professional.[12] Weston returned to Los Angeles, went to work for Louis A. Mojonier, and married Flora Chandler on January 30, 1909. Mojonier operated a thriving portrait studio in downtown Los Angeles, where Weston is believed to have worked for about two years, between about 1909 and 1911, first spotting negatives to remove blemishes and generally perfect the visage of the sitter, then advancing to the more creative and responsible position of photographer.

Among the skills Weston would have learned at the Illinois College of Photography was how to organize and run a one-man studio,[13] which was the most secure way of earning a

10 Charis Wilson, *Edward Weston Nudes* (Millerton, N.Y., 1977).

11 Michael Hargreaves, editor, *Tropico, The City Beautiful* (Los Angeles, 1916; facsimile, Los Angeles, 1986), 11.

12 Edward Weston, "Shall I Turn Professional," *American Photography* (November, 1912), 620-624. Repr. Bunnell, 8-10.

13 Edward Weston, "A One-Man Studio," *American Photography* (March, 1913), 130-134. Repr. Bunnell, 11-13.

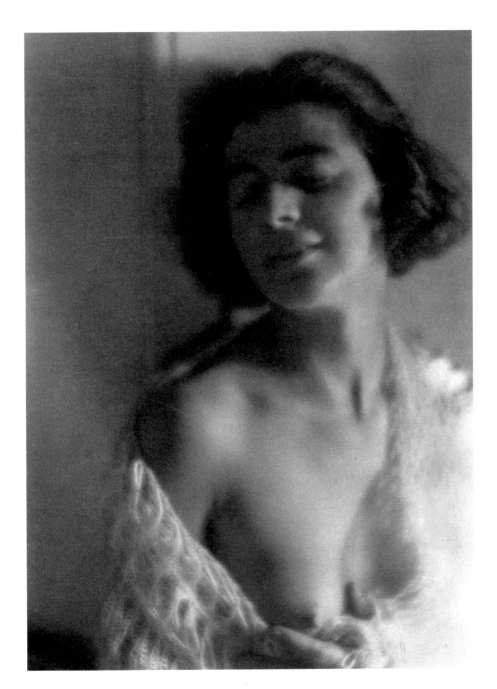

Plate 2.
Betty Brandner, 1920
The J. Paul Getty Museum.

Fig. 5.
*Retouching studio of Louis
A. Mojonier Studio* [?], Los
Angeles, 1908/1909
Private collection.

Fig. 6.
Archery Club, Los Angeles,
1909/1910
Private collection.

Fig. 7.
Nude Study [Flora
Weston], 1909/1910
Private collection.

Fig. 8.
Anne Brigman. *The
Brook,* from *Camera Work,*
January, 1909
The J. Paul Getty Museum.

Fig. 9.
*View from Tropico over
Griffith Park towards
Pacific Ocean,*
1908/1909
Private collection.

comfortable livelihood from photography. Weston became skilled at working without
assistance. Flora Chandler compiled an album of self-portraits of the two of them during
their courtship, where the exposure was made with a remote control device. Several group
portraits can be attributed to Weston, including one of the studio [Fig. 5], where Weston
himself is in the foreground, with the others arranged at their retouching consoles, light-
tables that used reflected window light to illuminate negatives from below.

During these years Weston continued to be active in archery, a sport in which his father also
had been active. Archery was a sport that trained the mind and brought the archer into
contact with ultimate reality, and according to one theorist of the subject brings the mind
into tune with the unconscious;[14] archery was part of Weston's indirect training for the art of
photography. On one occasion the artist made a self-portrait with his colleagues [Figs. 6,
15]. The placement of the targets, partially cropped out of the picture, and the interlocking
network of bows and arrows are ingenious compositional devices. The figure with the hands
on his shoulders is Edward Weston, who composed the photograph, leaving a place for
himself at the center, and then dashed in front of the camera while a remote control shutter
release did its work.

During 1909–1911 Weston continued to photograph on his own under the influence of the
circle of Alfred Stieglitz, with which he appears to have become familiar through *Camera
Work.* It is likely that Weston was introduced to this periodical in Chicago in 1908, since it
was only after this time that his work came to grips with the divergent stylistic possibilities
that existed on the international scene. In the same month that Weston married Flora
Chandler, Stieglitz devoted an entire issue of *Camera Work* to the photographs of Anne
Brigman (American, 1869–1950),[15] who was the only member of his Photo-Secession circle
living in California. Weston's earliest surviving nude, a study of Flora [Fig. 7], is in the
spirit of Brigman's *The Brook* [Fig. 8] and Alice Boughton's (American, 1866–1943) *Sand
and Wild Roses,* both of which were reproduced in *Camera Work* early in 1909. Weston
married an older woman and identified himself with two strong-willed female artists
(Brigman played the role of Sybil in Charles Keeler's "Will O' the Wisp" in 1908 and
Boughton attended a costume ball dressed as Queen Victoria).[16]

Late in 1909, following their marriage, Weston and his wife moved into their own house in
Tropico. Tropico, which called itself "The City Beautiful," was a bit of the Midwest or New
England transplanted to the Garden of Eden [Fig. 9]. The air was so clean that you could see
from the San Gabriel Mountains to the Pacific Ocean and the village had its own officer to

14 Eugen Herrigell,
*Zen in the Art of
Archery* (New
York, 1953), 9.

15 Therese Thau
Heyman, *Anne
Brigman Pictorial
Photographer/
Pagan/Member of
the Photo-Secession*
(Oakland
Museum, 1974).

16 Weston J. Naef,
"Anne W.
Brigman," in *The
Collection of Alfred
Stieglitz: Fifty
Pioneers of Modern
Photography* (New
York, 1978), 274,
278; Boughton's
*Sand and Wild
Roses* is reproduced
no. 65, 277.

ig. 10.
*nterior of first residence
*f Flora and Edward
Weston, Tropico, 1909
*rivate collection.

*ig. 11.
*Actor in Military Costume
*Mojonier Studio],
*909/1911
*rivate collection.

Fig. 12.
*Flora Weston and
Chandler Weston,
1910
*Private collection.

insure the absence of pestilence. Weston, who was reading *Physical Culture* magazine at the time, found the emphasis on healthy living very much to his liking. His and Flora's new home was a modest structure—more of a cottage than a house—[Fig. 10] built with an excellent understanding of the Arts and Crafts style recently introduced to California from the East Coast. Because Weston was a proficient photographer of interiors,[17] he was able to craft a tightly composed picture of his living environment, a picture carpentered with interlocking foreground and background elements. The walls are ornamented with photographs that may be lost examples of his own work.

Once he was promoted to the rank of photographer at the Mojonier studio in 1910 or 1911, Weston quickly demonstrated his superior ability at lighting and posing worthy citizens, vaudeville performers, and actors hoping to get in on the ground floor of the infant movie business. He created a living sculpture out of the figure of an unnamed actor in military costume [Fig. 11] who was posed and lighted so as to create a correct characterization.

A son, Edward Chandler Weston, was born to Edward and Flora in 1910, and another, Theodore Brett Weston, came along in 1911. Weston photographed his wife and sons with dedication as well as enthusiasm [Fig. 12]. The family photographs done for love are also experiments in lighting and posing.[18] Weston treated his wife and infant sons with a tenderness, affection, and pride that proved that he was a devoted family man. By 1912 Weston had resigned from his position with Louis Mojonier and established his own studio in Tropico.

The year 1912 was also important for Alfred Stieglitz, because in August he devoted an issue of *Camera Work* to the painting and sculpture of Picasso, and showed this work at the Photo-Secession Galleries, thus introducing modern art to America and establishing the yardstick by which all subsequent American art would be measured as avant-garde or traditional.[19]

The April issue of *Camera Work* was shared by Brigman and Karl Struss, and the October issue was devoted to Baron DeMeyer. Brigman represented the symbolist branch of modernism, which at the time was considered very progressive, but which in retrospect was actually more traditional, and was the preferred mode for experimental photographers such as Steichen,[20] who was responsible for introducing Stieglitz to modern European art. DeMeyer also represented a kind of avant-garde, for he was in the forefront of the movement to replace drawing as the principal vehicle for magazine illustration. Struss,[21] who himself moved to Los Angeles in 1919 but at this time lived in New York [Fig. 13], romanticized nature, but also showed a tendency toward symbolism in landscape.

17 Edward Weston, "Artistic Interiors," *Photo-Era* (December, 1911), 298-300. Repr. Bunnell, 1-3.

18 Edward Weston, "Photographing Children in the Studio," *American Photography* (February, 1912), 83-88. Repr. Bunnell, 4-7.

19 William I. Homer, *Alfred Stieglitz and the American Avant-Garde* (Boston, 1977).

20 Dennis Longwell, *Steichen, The Master Prints: The Symbolist Period* (Boston, 1978).

21 Bloomfield Hills, Cranbrook Academy of Art/ Museum, *Karl Struss: Man with a Camera,* January 13-February 15, 1976. Catalog essay by Susan and John Harvith.

Plate 3.
Betty Brandner, 1920
The J. Paul Getty Museum.

Fig. 13.
Karl Struss. *On the East
River, New York,* from
Camera Work, April, 1912
The J. Paul Getty Museum.

Fig. 14.
*Santa Monica Bay towards
Malibu,* ca. 1912
Private collection.

Fig. 15.
Woman with Bow,
1911/1912
Private collection.

Fig. 16.
Self-portrait [?],
1903/1904
Private collection.

Weston made a series of landscape studies that reflect Struss' style. In a view looking north across Santa Monica Bay toward Malibu [Fig. 14], geometric elements are introduced by the line of the mile-long pier and presented in ingenious counterpoint to the amorphous quality of the reflected light and the shadow of the mountains. As is typical of symbolist art, the photograph suggests meaning below the surface of the subject. In its concern for pure form—light and geometry—it was Weston's first acknowledgment that abstract elements could be the underlying basis for a photograph and that a photograph could be of value more for the relationships between its parts than for the subject represented. While such an attitude was in direct contradiction to that required of a photographer at the Mojonier Studio, it made perfect sense to Struss, whose photographs in the April 1911 *Camera Work* provide an excellent example of this type of composition. Struss and Weston struck up a friendship after Struss moved to Los Angeles and Weston made a striking portrait of him with his movie camera and special lights.

Between 1912 and 1915 Weston was looking at a contradictory variety of stylistic models and testing the relevance of various attitudes to his own artistic identity. He was attempting to resolve the divergent requirements of opposing visual premises in a way that mirrored the polygot of styles and subjects that Stieglitz had published in *Camera Work* and had believed in enough to collect for himself. A particularly fine portrait by Weston, believed to date from about 1913, shows a woman in a long dress, holding a bow and arrow standing on a rocky hill poised against a panoramic landscape [Fig. 15]. This photograph is an amalgam of contradictions—hard versus soft, passive versus assertive, figure versus landscape. The urge to reconcile opposites became a hallmark of Edward Weston's mature style. Archery was also an art of opposites that combined utilitarian purpose and aesthetic pleasure, and it provided Weston with a model to integrate the divergent aspects of the art of photography.

The years between 1911 and 1913 were also a time when Weston began to use his camera to ventilate a streak of healthy self-confidence that verged upon narcissism. He made numerous self-portraits, and they too combine contradictory motives. Even in his earliest surviving self-portrait of 1903, we see a young man whose self-image is that of a strong man, a doer and not a spectator [Fig. 16]. This image continues in the self-portrait with camera [Frontispiece] where Weston is dressed in the same type of outdoors gear he wore for railroad work [Fig. 3]. Later the photographer portrayed himself in a white shirt with sleeves rolled up in workaday fashion, signifying the shift from an outdoor to an indoor profession; the expression is neutral, earnest, and unemotional [Fig. 17]. By 1915 we see a different person. Destiny has begun to leave its mark, and plainness has been replaced by costume [Fig. 18].

Fig. 17.
Self-portrait,
1910/1912
Private collection.

Fig. 18.
Self-portrait, 1915
Private collection.

Fig. 19.
Portrait of My Son, ca. 1915
The J. Paul Getty Museum.

In a tweed hat and coat, Edward Weston is dressed for New York and not Los Angeles, much less the hamlet of Tropico where the photograph was made. Weston had begun to view himself as an urbane artist, but we also begin to see two Edward Westons, one motivated by duty (in shirtsleeves) and the other by imagination (in tweedy costume).

What had transpired in his life to make two personalities seem to grow in one body? In 1907, the year he was engaged to Flora, Weston appears to have been motivated by love; by 1909, after he had become a husband and father, the drive for security had begun to dominate and he had established a profession. In 1913–1914 the urge to be thought significant motivated his actions. Sometime between mid-1913 and mid-1914, Weston became even more ambitious and self-confident. In the spring of 1914, he wrapped five of his photographs (one of which is reproduced in Fig. 19), into a parcel and audaciously dispatched it to the jurors of the prestigious London Salon of Photography which—following the demise of the New York Photo-Secession in 1910—remained the most prestigious place in the world for photographs to be exhibited. Weston's photographs were singled out for commendation as the best pictures in the salon by Bertram Park, who was on the organizing committee and who commented, "Mr. Weston is evidently a man of original ideas, sound technique, a refined artistic perception, and a sense for decoration."[22]

The praise bestowed upon Weston for work displayed at the London Salon brought immediate response and by early 1915, when the article had filtered back across the Atlantic, unexpected visitors began to appear at his doorstep. Among the first was a writer named J. C. Thomas, who found his way to Tropico to interview the photographer whom he later depicted as a bohemian fugitive from urban life who had no use for power or money. Thomas put his finger on the nonconformist aspects of Weston's personality:

Out in the town of Tropico, a beautiful suburb of Los Angeles, stands a shack studio of rough boarding that is so full of art that its range of influence reaches to the ends of the earth. In that studio, which cost perhaps six hundred dollars to build, dreams and works Edward H. Weston, 'photographer', as the simple mission-style, brown-stained sign hanging in front of the door announces.[23]

By the summer of 1915 Edward Weston had gathered a basketful of laurels. In the fall of 1916 there was an article on his work by Sidney Allan,[24] who had also published criticism under the name Sadakichi Hartmann and who had been one of the strongest critical voices during the heyday of the New York Photo-Secession. Weston had enough work to require assistance; a strong-willed young woman named Margrethe Mather filled the bill to insure

22 "A Symposium: Which is the Best Picture at the London Salon?" *Amateur Photographer and Cinematographer* (29 September 1914), 250. Repr. Newhall and Conger, 2-3; 3.

23 J.C. Thomas, "A David Grayson Kind of Man," *American Magazine* (August, 1915), 55-56. Repr. Newhall and Conger, 4-6; 4.

24 Sidney Allan, "Looking for the Good Points," *Bulletin of Photography* (November, 1916), 472-473. Repr. Newhall and Conger, 9-10.

ate 4.
na Modotti, 1921
he J. Paul Getty Museum.

Plate 5.
Paul Jordan-Smith, 1922
The J. Paul Getty Museum.

that portraits from the Weston studio were marked with individuality and correct characterization that he felt were lacking in "picture factories" like the Mojonier establishment. When his sister asked him why he had decided to locate his studio in the suburb of Tropico rather than in downtown Los Angeles, he replied, "Sis, I'm going to make my name so famous that it won't matter where I live."[25]

By 1915 Weston had become a pillar of the city of Tropico. The photographic illustrations in a forty-four page guidebook promotional brochure about the city were by "E.H. Weston," whose studio merited a chapter following the one on Society, Clubs, and Lodges. The text paraphrased one of Weston's own early articles in saying that "his work is not merely the product of a picture taking machine, but of an artist's brain and skill,"[26] and he was credited with bringing many prominent artists to Tropico.

In 1915 Weston traveled to San Francisco to see the Panama-Pacific International Exposition. The trip left a deep impression on him. Here he saw avant-garde paintings from Europe, apparently for the first time, and met a group of "radical new friends [who] introduced him to contemporary thought, music, literature."[27] Weston already knew about Cézanne, Rodin, Picasso, Matisse, and other protagonists of the modern movement through reproductions in *Camera Work* and other art magazines, but he apparently had not seen the works of art themselves before 1915 nor had he met people who could speak articulately about modernism. What he saw was the first group of Italian Futurist paintings and sculptures ever shown in the United States as well as paintings by Oskar Kokoschka and Edvard Munch.[28] Publications issued to commemorate the exhibition included a "Catalog Deluxe" in which an essay by Boccioni entitled "The Italian Futurist Painting and Sculpture: Initiators of the Futuristic Art" was translated.[29] The Expressionist and Symbolist paintings, however, left more of an impression on him than the Futurists. Among the photographs he saw, those of Brigman, Struss, and White left the deepest impression on him and he said so in a lecture to a Los Angeles group in 1916.[30] The influence of modernism began to be felt in Weston's work about 1916, but it was the symbolist and expressionist path and not that of Cubism that first attracted him.

It is also possible that Weston actually met Anne Brigman in San Francisco in 1915. In that year he photographed several dancers including Yvonne Sinnard, Violet Romer [Fig. 20], and Ted Shawn. Dance was at the heart of Brigman's photography,[31] and she may have introduced Weston to it. After separating from her husband in 1910, she had established a close friendship with Alfred Stieglitz, who promised to show her work at the Photo-

25 Charis Wilson, "Family Portrait," in Kathy Kelsey Foley, *Edward Weston's Gifts to his Sister* (Dayton Art Institute, 1978), 17.

26 Hargreaves, [29-30].

27 Nancy Newhall, *Edward Weston* (New York, 1946). Repr. Newhall and Conger, 79-86; 80.

29 John E.D. Trask and J. Nilson Laurvik, *Catalog Deluxe of the Department of Fine Arts Panama-Pacific International Exposition* (San Francisco, 1915), 123-127.

28 Peter C. Bunnell, "Weston in 1915," letter to the Editor, *Afterimage* 3 (December, 1975): 16-17. Repr. Newhall and Conger, 175-178; 176.

30 Edward Weston, "Photography as a Means of Artistic Expression," lecture, College Women's Club, Los Angeles, October 18, 1916. Manuscript, Weston-Hagemeyer Collection, Center for Creative Photography, University of Arizona. Repr. Bunnell, 18-21; 18.

31 Naef, nos. 97, 98, 283.

Fig. 20.
Violet Romer, 1915
The Museum of Modern Art, New York.

Secession Galleries (the exhibition did not materialize). Brigman, who was half a generation older than Weston, focused almost exclusively on the nude figure in a wild landscape; her photographs project a libertine spirit and suggest hidden meaning. In collaboration with Francis Bruguière she organized an exhibition of photographs for the 1915 Pan-Pacific Exposition in which Weston's work was included. Brigman lived in a tiny house with a red dog and an aviary of birds that was the locus of San Francisco's most authentic salon for literati,[32] and it is in this context that Weston, the most celebrated photographer of Southern California, would have met his colleagues from the North.

32 Heyman, 8.

Ever a purist at heart, Weston attempted in his photographs of dancers to convey the essence of movement by relying on standard photographic procedures, which at the time included the soft-focus lens and various forms of scrim used in lighting to soften edges and create spatial and planar ambiguity. Although he was apparently fascinated by the Futurist art he saw in San Francisco, he did not adopt futurist methods literally. For instance, he avoided procedures like multiple exposure or the sandwiching of negatives that were used by Italian photographers at this time. There is, however, an intrinsic connection between Futurist art and the element of motion that Weston attempted to signify in his dance photographs.

Many years later Weston severely criticized his work of this period, calling it a time in which he was trying to be "artistic": "I even dressed the part," he recalled, "windsor tie, green velvet jacket—see, I was an artist."[33] It is tantalizing to think that Brigman, the most theatrical of the photographers collected by Alfred Stieglitz, became his mentor and led him toward a self-image of the photographer as a dramatic artificer. Since her fervent correspondence with Stieglitz ended abruptly in 1918, we are left wondering whether Weston had replaced him as the object of Brigman's interest. Brigman is believed to have moved to Los Angeles about 1918, but her biography for this period suddenly becomes as opaque as Weston's.

33 *Daybooks I*, xviii.

Between 1917 and 1920 Edward Weston was concerned with photographs that were intelligent by the yardstick of rational thought. He wrote that a photograph can only be as good as the eye and the mind behind the camera: "As great a picture can be made as one's own mental capacity—no greater."[34] Weston was attempting to define for himself whether the higher order of intelligence was that of the unconscious mind or that of the mind at its most rational.

34 Edward Weston, "Portraiture," *Photo-Miniature* (September, 1917), 354-356. Repr. Bunnell, 22.

Two portraits of Johan Hagemeyer tell much about Weston's stylistic evolution during

Plate 6.
Imogen Cunningham, 1922
The J. Paul Getty Museum.

Fig. 21.
Johan Hagemeyer, ca. 1918
Center for Creative
Photography.

Fig. 22.
Johan Hagemeyer [as
Jean Christophe], ca. 1920
The Oakland Museum.

Fig. 23.
Epilogue, 1918
Private collection.

Fig. 24.
Anne Brigman. *The Heart
of the Storm,* ca. 1915
The Metropolitan Museum
of Art, The Alfred Stieglitz
Collection, 1933.

38 Maddow, 42.

this period. It is unclear how Weston and Hagemeyer met, but it may have been before Hagemeyer's Eastern sojourn of 1916-1917, because when he returned to Los Angeles in 1917, the two men were already good enough friends that he stayed in Tropico with the Westons. The first portrait [Fig. 21] dating from 1918, shows Hagemeyer leaning against a window with his pipe in his mouth and hands in his pockets and is related stylistically to the 1915/1916 Romer and Shawn dance pieces in its soft-focus tonality and concern for instinctive compositional elements. The second Hagemeyer portrait of 1920 shows him posed frontally with cape and walking stick and lit by a bright flood in the studio corner [Fig. 22] playing the fictional role of Jean Christophe. The style of his image again suggests the influence of Brigman. The arrangement of furniture, lighting, and pose promote a sense of highly stylized drama, and it is this enigmatic quality, missing in other Weston photographs of this period, that pervaded Brigman's art. A comparable sense of enigma created by stylized pose and eccentric lighting characterizes Weston's *Epilogue* of 1918 [Fig. 23], a work that genuinely baffled the public when it was reproduced the following year. William A. French, editor of *Photo-Era,* wrote of this photograph: "It is, perhaps, idle to speculate as to the artist's intent which may have [been] none other than to create something strikingly unconventional, based upon a plausible theory of design."[35] About 1919 Weston began to assign titles to his work that added an explicit literary dimension to the visual one. He had an excellent command of language, but the phrasing of some of his titles is out of character with his earlier practice and may reflect Brigman's predilecton for fanciful titles.[36] Typical are Brigman's *The Spider's Web* (1908) and *The Heart of the Storm* (ca. 1915) [Fig. 24], photographs that bear comparison for their titles to Weston's *Epilogue,* and to its counterpart, *Prologue to a Sad Spring* (1920). Weston's *Bathers* of 1919 [Pl. 1] recalls Brigman's *The Pool* of 1912. In his bathing-pool series Weston concerns himself with the overriding concern for light and a compositional formula in which the parts are tied together by an interlocking network of lines and shapes, while Brigman, on the other hand, was almost wholly concerned with literary content and expression.

By 1921 Weston knew Brigman well enough to photograph her in the nude and to create a photograph that projects tenderness and emotion as well as objectivity [Fig. 25].[37] Just one photograph can be securely identified with Brigman as the model, but it could not have been the only exposure nor does the existence of but a single photograph necessarily suggest that Brigman and Weston met on just one occasion. In 1921 Brigman closed a letter to him that was full of familiarities with a phrase that suggests meaning between the lines: "Aloha to Flora and the kiddies from Uncle Anne...much love for yourself."[38] Between 1915/1917, when it has been suggested that Weston met Brigman (and began the diaries that he later

35 Maddow, 41.

36 Brigman's lyric sensibility is anthologized in her self-published book of poems, *Songs of a Pagan,* 1949.

37 Amy Conger sees a connection between Brigman and Weston: Monterey Peninsula Museum of Art, *The Monterey Photographic Tradition: The Weston Years* (1986), 19, as does Mike Weaver in *The Photographic Art: Pictorial Traditions in Britain and America* (New York, 1986), 96-97, where Brigman is characterized as a dedicated Symbolist while "Weston became a vitalist." It should also be noted that about 1915 Weston began to elongate the "W" in his name in a very mannered way that echoes the formation of Brigman's middle initial as she signed it on her photographs.

Fig. 25.
Nude Study [Anne Brigman], 1921
Division of Photographic
History, National
Museum of American
History.

destroyed), and 1922, when it is likewise postulated that the relationship ended (and around the time the surviving diaries commence again), Weston's attitudes changed profoundly. His art began to alternate between soft-focus and hard edge; between artifice and naturalism; and between emotionally neutral and emotionally charged styles. Clearly he was lost in a world carried deep within himself and was attempting to sort out contradictory possibilities.

The ambivalence Weston experienced appears to have been the result of the influence of a combination of forces. One influence on him was Margrethe Mather, who was advancing from volunteer assistant to partner in the studio. She loved all-night parties and fraternized with a circle of artists and intellectuals. Ben Maddow, who believes they met as early as 1912, describes the person and the relationship as follows: "...Small, very pretty, and exceptionally intelligent...she was mostly, though not wholly, a lesbian [and] Edward Weston fell desperately in love with her."[39] The issues for Weston at this time in his life and in his art were experiment versus formula, excitement versus boredom, and intellectual versus pedestrian values.

39 Maddow, 41.

His treatment of the nude is one of the keys to Weston's stylistic and personal growth. His first nudes were of female models and started with the 1909 study of Flora [Fig. 7]. Around 1916 or 1917 he began a series of figure studies with Margrethe Mather as his model. For the most part these broke no new ground and were a reference to Clarence White and Alfred Stieglitz's Cramer-Thomson series of 1907.[40] Weston made at least three studies of Mather—posed with props in the form of drapery or vases with flower arrangements using a soft-focus lens on his camera [Fig. 26]. Another model who posed nude for him in 1920 was Betty Brandner [Pl. 2], who is shown somewhat more suggestively in a lacy shawl with her fingers to her breast and eyes closed as though indulging in a private fantasy.

40 Naef, nos. 560-563, 490-493.

Fig. 26.
Nude Study, ca. 1919
The J. Paul Getty Museum.

In 1919 Weston became interested in a new subject, the male nude. Around 1912 or 1913 he had already photographed his two-year-old son Chandler nude both frontally and from the back, photographs that show great attention to placement of the camera, lighting, and composition, as well as to the human form [Fig. 27]. Weston apparently did not return to the male figure until about 1919, when he did a series of photographs of boys skinny-dipping in the bathing pool of Paul Jordan-Smith's house in Claremont [Pl. 1]. The surviving photographs from this series show different strategies of picturemaking. In one, shadows cast against the back wall and the rippling reflections draw attention away from the figures; in another the geometry of the pool-edge and the compositional tension between the gymnast's rings at the upper right corner and fingers of the boy at the left—trimmed exactly

Fig. 27.
Chandler Weston, ca. 1912
Private collection.

Plate 7.
Plaster Works, 1925
Private collection.

Fig. 28.
Neil Weston, 1923
International Museum of
Photography at George
Eastman House.

to the paper's edge—are signals that Weston was interested in more than the nude male form. He seems here to have been asking himself these questions: how do I relate to these particular subjects? how do the subjects relate to their context? and how do the parts relate to the whole?

In 1923 Weston posed his son Neil at the age of eight for nude studies [Fig. 28] that very tenderly, but sensually, explore the beauties of the male torso photographed at the same close range as Betty Brandner had been photographed in 1920. During the course of 1920-1921, Weston's treatment of the nude became increasingly adventurous and erotic, leading to the photographs he made of Brigman in 1921.[41] Her face shown in just one of these supplies the identity of the model. Weston moved his camera closer to the subject than ever before, focusing the lens obliquely into Brigman's armpit and breast; her forearm covers her eyes in a gesture closer to anxiety or remorse than to contentment [Fig. 25]. In this photograph Weston stepped boldly over the line that separates veiled eroticism from blatant sexuality.

Does the Brigman photograph of 1921 provide any clue as to how long they may have known each other? The photograph communicates a sense of intimate familiarity between the thirty-four-year-old Weston and fifty-year-old Brigman and is surely the product of an association in which the physical and emotional distance between the photographer and his model was reduced to nil. A candid relationship could not have been established overnight, even by someone as charismatic as Weston. Just how their friendship began as well as how it ended remain a mystery, but we know he came actually to dislike the photographs made under Brigman's influence even when logic and the opinions of others were to the contrary. For example, Alfred Stieglitz commented favorably when they met for the first time in 1922, saying, "This breast is perhaps the most complete thing you have."[42] Twenty-five years later, around 1947, Weston made an addendum to this remark in the first pages of the surviving journal: "I know this photo was full of striving for effect, sensational, one of the least important prints I showed [to Stieglitz]."[43]

During the summer of 1919, perhaps through Ruth St. Denis, Weston made the acquaintance of a former dancer, Clarence B. McGehee, who was also known as "Ramiel."[44] Weston's male nudes coincide exactly with the start and flourishing of his friendship with McGehee, who was a homosexual,[45] and suggest that the photographer was asking himself through his photographs questions about the particular beauties of the male form.

One year after Weston so intimately photographed Anne Brigman, he also portrayed Ramiel

41 Anne Brigman is listed as a subject in Weston's register of negatives (Edward Weston Archives, Center for Creative Photography, The University of Arizona); however, the list is not complete for the names of his models. Just one print with the model securely identified as Brigman is known (Figure 25). Several other studies of single breasts made at this time are directly related works, and may represent Brigman as the model.

42 *Daybooks I*, 6.

43 *Daybooks I*, 6.

44 Maddow, 44.

45 Dody Weston Thompson, "Edward Weston," *Malahat Review* (April, 1970), 39-80. Rept. Newhall and Conger, 132-151; 144.

Fig. 29.
Ramiel in His Attic, 1920
The Oakland Museum.

McGehee in the attic of his mother's house in Redondo Beach [Fig. 29], creating a masterpiece of cool, unemotional formalism. The composition may be compared to that of *Bathers* of 1919 [Pl. 1], where a similar network of lines, shapes, and reflections directs our attention away from the nude figures, and to that of *Betty in Her Attic* [Pl. 3] of the year before. In the photograph of Ramiel a geometric network establishes a very hard-edged form with rather pliant still-life details at the edges, a carefully constructed context into which the head of the sitter is placed as though it were another element of the still life, an object to be seen but not touched. *Ramiel in His Attic* is important because the image carried Weston's concern for complete integration of form and content much farther than the *Bathers*. Ramiel is treated as a figure to be woven seamlessly into the warp and woof of its context. The composition has more to do with Cézanne than with Picasso, and it owes more to Constructivism than to Cubism. *Ramiel in His Attic* was immediately praised by such knowledgeable viewers as Imogen Cunningham, who wrote to Weston,

It's brains, pure brains, and intellect all over the photographic surface.... If it doesn't make old near-sighted Stieglitz sit up and look around...I don't know what could. It has Paul Strand's eccentric efforts...put to shame, because it is more than eccentric. It has all of the cubistically inclined photographers laid low.[46]

46 Maddow, 43.

During 1920 and 1921 Weston photographed dancers and performers drawn from the world of dance on several occasions. The most interesting of these series represents a Japanese theatrical company. An untitled study shows a figure in a Japanese fighting mask that largely conceals the face of the performer. The single-point light source and enigmatic content relate this image to *Epilogue* of three years later [Fig. 23]; in both of these works we see an echo of Brigman's symbolism. However, there is also a concern for the geometrics of formal composition. We see as well Weston moving closer to his subject, as he had done in the Brigman nude. In so doing, Weston manifested his personal fascination with a subject that suggests violence and retribution; form and emotion are associated by metaphor and not by declaration.

47 Maddow, 46.

Weston met Tina Modotti and her husband, Roubaix de l'Abrie Richey, in 1919. He soon established a particularly close friendship with Modotti, another in the line of important strong-willed women in his life.[47] Roubaix was a textile designer, as was another close friend of Weston, George Stojana, whose batik designs were used by Weston as studio backdrops in 1921-1922. Modotti, who was a talented photographer, became one of Weston's favorite models in 1921. In one of the earliest of his pictures of her, Modotti is posed in a composition

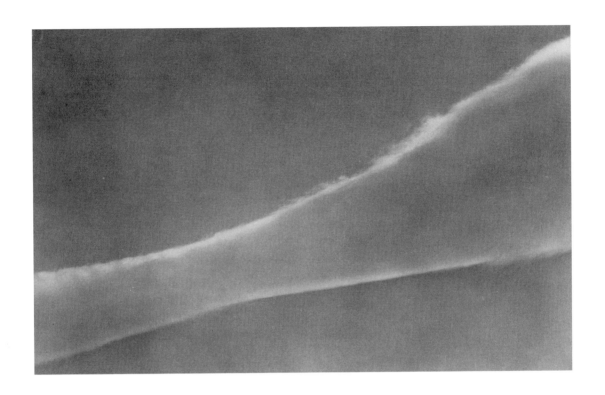

Plate 8.
Cloud, Mexico, 1926
The J. Paul Getty Museum.

related to the Hagemeyer portrait of 1920, with the hanging batik and trunk replacing the tall chest of drawers and chair. Weston moved his camera closer and closer to Modotti [Pl. 4] as if to telegraph a deepening of their relationship, which developed into a torrid romance in 1921. The consummation of this affair was recorded by Modotti in a letter to Weston that is more explicit than those which survive from his relationships with Mather or Brigman:

With tenderness I speak your name over and over to myself—in a way that brings you nearer to me tonight as I sit here alone remembering.... Last night—this hour you were reading to me from an exquisite volume—or were we sipping wine and smoking—or had darkness enveloped us and were you—the memory of this thrills me to the point of swooning!—tell me, were you at this hour— kissing my left breast? Oh! the beauty of it all! Wine—books—pictures—music—candlelight— eyes to look into—and then darkness—and kisses—[48]

48 Amy Stark, *The Letters from Tina Modotti to Edward Weston,* monograph number 21 (January, 1986) of *The Archive,* a serial publication of the Center for Creative Photography, University of Arizona, 14.

In 1922 Edward Weston's life changed dramatically with his first trip East[49] since 1908. His initial objective was to see his sister, May Seaman, who had moved from Tropico to Middletown, Ohio, and other relatives including his Aunt Emma and Uncle Theodore in Chicago. While in Ohio, Weston made a vast leap away from his recent subjects when he decided to photograph around the Armco steel mill in Middletown [Fig. 30] where his brother-in-law, John Seaman, worked. Weston had photographed few landscapes or other outdoor subjects in the preceding decade. In Los Angeles, Weston passed oil refineries on the way to Redondo Beach, and may have known the Kaiser steel works in Fontana, but there was no truly comparable industrial monument of similarly impressive dimensions in South-ern California; it comes as no surprise that Weston would have studied the blast furnaces as a rare species. He treated the metal pipes and towers with the same reverence that European photog-raphers such as Frederick Evans[50] (whose photographs of York Minster and Ely Cathedral were reproduced in *Camera Work*) treated the Gothic cathedral. With the sure hand of a gifted draftsman Weston delineated the edges and shapes, highlights and shadows of the alien industrial forms as though he had been observing them all of his life. Their thrusting stacks are an important artistic step towards the language of symbolic rather than literal forms.

49 *Daybooks I,* 4-8; See also "Weston to Hagemeyer: New York Notes," *Center for Creative Photography* 3 (November, 1976).

50 "Letter Regarding Pictorialist Practices in Response to Comments by F.H. Evans," *American Photography* (August, 1922), 533-534. Repr. Bunnell, 24-25.

Although Edward Weston was broke, his sister felt strongly that he should visit New York to meet the photographers whose work he had admired in *Camera Work*. The Tropico portrait studio was not financially successful, but with money from May and Tina Modotti, Weston left for New York. His companion on this odyssey was "Jo," who has been tentatively identified as Ruth Wilton,[51] a woman who had modeled for him in Los Angeles and who remains as shadowy as Brigman in his biography.

51 Maddow, 48.

Weston dutifully recorded his conversations with Alfred Stieglitz, noting that he was well received and was given constructive criticism ("frankly, I did not always know what he was talking about").[52] He noted verbatim some of Stieglitz's comments including those on his favorites among Weston's compositions. Stieglitz showed Weston two of his own nude studies of Georgia O'Keeffe, the woman he fell in love with in 1917 and married in 1921 after divorcing his first wife. Although Stieglitz was twenty years Weston's senior, he was experiencing at almost the same time the trauma of being out of step with the old and in need of something new. Weston remembered Stieglitz's words to him and was able to write them verbatim in his journal:

Friends made me out a god, when all I asked was to be treated as a human being, then turned on me when I couldn't be all they asked. . . . [now] I have nothing left, deserted by friends and wife and child—yet in no period of my life have I been so enthusiastic and interested in photography and anxious to work. . . . If you had come to me four years ago [before meeting O'Keeffe] I should not have been ripe to give you what I do now.[53]

Weston's comment in his journal after quoting this passage was, "Nor I ripe to receive [this advice]."

Weston returned to Los Angeles late in 1922 apparently resolved to burn bridges. He decided to destroy almost the entire journal he had written prior to his meeting with Stieglitz, which was tantamount to saying that he finally had found in Stieglitz the artistic role model that suited his temperament. It was a style of art and a mental attitude towards the purposes of art that dramatically differed from Brigman's.

Not too many weeks after his return he was visited in Tropico by Johan Hagemeyer, who saw for the first time his friend's photograph of the Armco mill. Hagemeyer was so ecstatic over the beauty of this picture that he declared, according to Weston's journal, "I have never before demanded a print from you Edward—but I must have a copy of that. . . . It is a thing I wish I had made—but I am glad you made it for me to enjoy—for I feel I *could* have done it."[54]

Between 1921 and 1923 Weston photographed with a new sense of probing the depths of character; most of his subjects were friends, who became the guinea pigs for artistic experiments. He avoided the figure-ground problem that he was exploring in the attic series with Betty Brandner and Ramiel McGehee and attempted to record the essence of

52 *Daybooks I, 4.*

53 *Daybooks I, 5.*

Fig. 30.
Armco Steel, 1922
Private collection.

54 *Daybooks I, 10.*

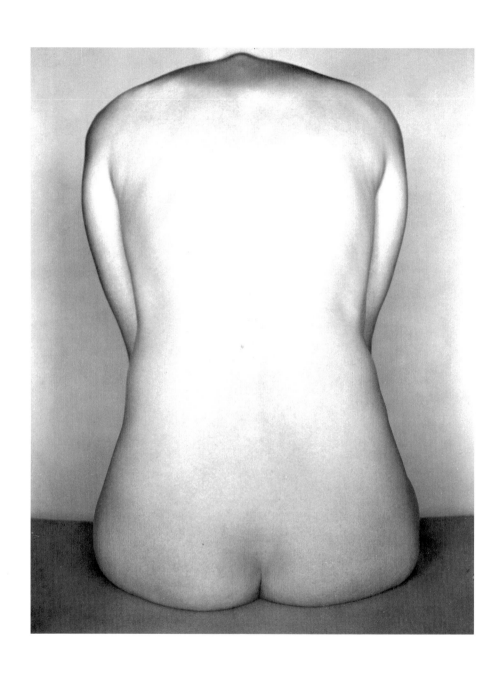

Plate 9.
Nude [Cristal Gang], 1927
The J. Paul Getty Museum.

personality in the flash of recognition that photography makes possible by shortening the distance between the hand and the eye. His portraits, beginning with the frontal Tina Modotti [Pl. 4] and continuing through Paul Jordan-Smith smoking a cigarette [Pl. 5] and Imogen Cunningham in profile [Pl. 6], are studies in pure perception. They represent the photographer's ability to move in close and fill the frame with arrangements of light and dark, line and pattern, shape and void, pose and gesture—the fundamental building blocks of form visualized with emotion. They are photographs with no easily describable compositional features and are the result of instinct rather than design, the product of the unconscious and intuitive part of the mind rather than its seat of rationality.

55 Paul Jordan-Smith, *Bibliographia Burtoniana: a Study of Robert Burton's, The Anatomy of Melancholy, with a Bibliography of Burton's Writings* (Stanford, 1931).

Paul Jordan-Smith, who was a university professor and bibliophile, influenced Weston greatly.[55] When they met, Smith had achieved some celebrity for his 1916 book *The Soul of Women: An Interpretation of the Philosophy of Feminism,* a treatise that may have fascinated Weston because of his predilection for strong-willed, independent-minded women. Smith was well versed in psychology and the literature of the occult and had a strong interest in the Renaissance notion of melancholy, an emotion which Weston was experiencing in 1920. It may just be a coincidence that around 1920, when he met Paul Jordan-Smith, Weston's photographs took a decidedly intuitive turn, and he began to focus on recording states of mind rather than countenances. But it is more likely that Smith introduced Weston to the literature of psychology and the occult, and that what he learned reinforced thoughts that had already begun subconsciously to percolate through his mind.

There were also external reasons for Weston's melancholia. Between 1913 and 1916 he had earned by his own count thirty awards, recognitions, and exhibitions for his photographs. By 1916 he had ascended to a high pinnacle with a view straight down as well as one to the horizon. If he expected the accolades to continue rolling in he was mistaken, for after Sadakichi Hartmann's article in the fall of 1916, there was but one notable piece of writing on his work until Rafael Vera de Cordova's 1922 article in Spanish. Weston had temporarily lost his audience, which in Los Angeles was reduced to intellectuals and foreigners. He sold more photographs to Japanese tradesmen during a show arranged by Ramiel McGehee at the Shaku-Do-Sha, a men's social club, than to the pillars of Los Angeles' art establishment.[56]

56 Maddow, 46.

In 1923 Weston left Los Angeles for Mexico accompanied by Tina Modotti, much as Gauguin had abandoned France for Tahiti thirty years before. He wrote home regularly but his heart was elsewhere, and when he returned to Los Angeles in 1925/1926 for a six-month interlude, distance had taken its toll on his relationships with family and friends. His creative spirits were very high, however, and while in Los Angeles he made a series of photographs of a plaster mill which is as important as any he made in Mexico and which relates directly to the Armco photographs of three years earlier. The genius of *Plaster Works* [Pl. 7] is that static architecture is endowed with animus of the subtlest kind. If the Armco stacks are the epitome of male instincts, *Plaster Works* evokes the essence of the female in a most unexpected way. There is first the animus of a composition that is totally intuitive and that lacks any suggestion of academic geometries of the kind we saw in *Ramiel in His Attic* [Fig. 29]. *Plaster Works* is a composition realized from elements as simple and public as the clouds that so interested Stieglitz, and to which Weston first addressed himself in Mexico [Pl. 8], doubtless inspired by Stieglitz's example.

When Weston returned permanently to California from Mexico in late 1926 he was involved with an internalized universe. His personal objective was the representation of archetypes, of which he found one expression in the human figure [Pl. 9] and another in still-life arrangements of bananas [Pl. 10] and shells. Los Angeles was the locus of these particularly important studies. In the spring of 1927 he wrote a paragraph in his journal that eloquently translates into words what he had been seeking in his photographs since the early twenties, and that verbally signified attainment of his goal:

To clearly express my feeling for life with photographic beauty, present objectively the texture, rhythm, form in nature, without subterfuge or evasion in technique or spirit, to record the quintessence of the object or element before my lens, rather than an interpretation, a superficial phase, or passing mood—this is my way in photography. [57]

57 Edward Weston, "From My Day Book," *Creative Art* (August, 1928), xxix-xxxvi. Repr. Bunnell, 48-52; 51.

As an afterthought he added: "It is not an easy way." Weston had come to believe that photography had been devitalized by the impressionism Anne Brigman and other pictorialist photographers stood for, and he turned his back on their example forever.

Weston J. Naef

34

Plate 10.
Still Life with Bananas and Orange], 1927
The J. Paul Getty Museum.

Titles/dates, except those in brackets which we have assigned, are those inscribed by the artist, or are names of identified sitters. Unless otherwise stated, all items are from the collection of The J. Paul Getty Museum.

1   *Courtship of Flora Chandler and Edward Weston.* Gelatin silver. [1909]. Private collection

2   *View of Tropico.* Gelatin silver, [1908-09]. Private collection

3   *Flora Weston.* Gelatin silver, 1909. Private collection

4   [*Santa Monica Bay*]. Gelatin silver, [1912]. Private collection

5   *Costume Study* [*The Goldfish*]. Platinum, 1916. 85.XM.170.1

6   *Yvonne Sinnard.* Gelatin silver, 1916. 85.XM.403.1

7   *Sadakichi Hartmann.* Platinum, 1917. 85.XM.250.3

8   *John Cowper Powys.* Gelatin silver, 1918. 85.XM.257.5

9   *Bathers.* Gelatin silver, 1919. 85.XM.257.1

10   [*Standing Nude*]. Gelatin silver, [1919]. 85.XM.257.3

11   *Betty Brandner.* Gelatin silver, 1920. 85.XM.170.12

12   *Betty* [*Brandner*] *in Her Attic.* Gelatin silver, 1920. 85.XM.170.10

13   *Betty Brandner.* Gelatin silver, 1920. 85.XM.170.8

14   *Betty Brandner.* Gelatin silver, 1920. 85.XM.170.3

15   *Chandler Weston.* Platinum, 1920. Private collection

16   *Johan Hagemeyer* [as Jean Christophe]. Gelatin silver, 1920. The Oakland Museum

In no period of my life has there been a comparable series of important events coming one upon another as if to crowd into ten years all that might happen to some in a lifetime. I doubt if I can take time to recall more than the highlights of these years, or scratch the surface of all the changes which in turn have changed me, colored my thoughts, directed my actions.[1]

1 Edward Weston, *The Daybooks* (Rochester, 1961), 2: 287.

When Edward Weston resumed the keeping of his daybooks or diaries in 1944, after a hiatus of ten years, he sought to recall the memorable events, both personal and professional, of the preceding decade. Among the most significant were his move from Carmel to Santa Monica in 1935, friendship and later marriage to Charis Wilson, and in 1937 and 1938 work on a Guggenheim grant, the first ever awarded a photographer. Weston also published two books, *California and the West* in 1940 and an edition of Walt Whitman's *Leaves of Grass* in 1941, illustrated with photographs taken on his extensive travels across America during this productive period in his career.

Weston's original application for the Guggenheim grant in October of 1936 consisted of a single paragraph:

I wish to continue an epic series of photographs of the West, begun about 1929; this will include a range from satires on advertising to ranch life, from beach kelp to mountains. The publication of the above seems assured.[2]

2 See Weston's Guggenheim Scrapbook in the Archives of the Center for Creative Photography, (hereafter referred to as Scrapbook B). Portions of the application have also been republished in *Edward Weston on Photography*, ed. Peter Bunnell (Salt Lake City, 1983), 78.

It is obvious, from even this brief outline, that Weston thought his photographs in the late 1930s were an extension of his earlier work. And the present exhibition includes a broad range of photographs, from detailed still-life studies to panoramic landscapes.

All of these photographs come from a collection given by Weston to the Huntington Library between 1940 and 1944. The Guggenheim Foundation agreed to extend his original grant for a second year and later provided the funds to cover the costs of printing this set of photographs. The collection of five hundred prints represented, at the time, the largest holding of Weston's work in a public collection and, furthermore, it was one of Weston's earliest attempts to present a synopsis of his photographic career.

Weston's statement to the Guggenheim Foundation points to several significant aspects of the Huntington's holdings. First it should be noted that, although the principal portion of the collection is made up of work done between 1937 and 1941, Weston also selected examples of his earlier work which he felt related to his more recent photographs. It is very

Plate 11.
White Radish, 1933
The Henry E. Huntington
Library and Art Gallery.

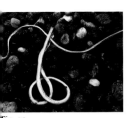

clear from his correspondence with the Guggenheim Foundation that he viewed this series as an extension of his earlier still-life and landscape work at Carmel in the early thirties.[3]

3 I wish to thank Stephen Schlesinger, Secretary of the Guggenheim Foundation, who provided access to the correspondence between Weston and Henry Allen Moe at the Foundation.

In choosing prints for the Huntington gift, Weston included about twenty works produced between 1927 and 1936: several Mexican studies, vegetable [Pl. 11] and shell still-lifes [Fig. 31], and details of plants and rocks done at Point Lobos [Fig. 32]. Many of these images have proved to be among his most popular works. While he continued to produce close-up studies of nature throughout his career [Pl. 12], there is a shift in emphasis in the Guggenheim period away from the details of nature to more expansive views of the landscape. [Pls. 13 and 20].[4]

4 John Szarkowski's introduction to the 1975 Museum of Modern Art exhibition remains the best characterization of this period in Weston's career, see "Edward Weston's Later Work," reprinted in *Edward Weston Omnibus,* ed. Beaumont Newhall and Amy Conger (Salt Lake City, 1984), 158-159.

A second feature of Weston's Guggenheim work is the broader range of material he included and his tendency to select subjects that can be defined in terms of contrast. In an addendum to the Guggenheim application, Weston elaborated on the significance of his choice of subject matter:

My work-purpose, my theme, can most nearly be stated as the recognition, recording and presentation of the interdependence, the relativity of all things—the universality of basic form.... In a single day's work, within the radius of a mile, I might discover and record the skeleton of a bird, a blossoming fruit tree, a cloud, a smokestack; each of these being only a part of a whole, but each—in itself—becoming a symbol of the whole, of life.[5]

5 Letter to Moe 2/4/37, Scrapbook B.

In this summary Weston presents a series of objects in juxtaposition: subjects seen as opposites representing death and life, the natural and man-made. For the viewer and the photographer alike, meaning is derived not only from the individual photograph, but also from the relationship of one image to another. Thus the Huntington's photographs are especially important because they represent not only a collective vision of Weston's work, but also one that the artist himself conceived.

Finally, in Weston's desire to see his photographs published in book form, there exists an important link with the documentary photographic movement of the 1930s. The Guggenheim grant provided Weston with the artistic freedom and financial backing that allowed him to work as he wished. His chosen mode of production—that is, traveling by car cross-country, gathering a vast reservoir of imagery, and then selecting particular prints for publication—was not unlike the methods used by the government-sponsored photographers working for the Farm Security Administration (FSA) during this period.[6]

6 Weston traveled over 22,000 miles, shooting on average 8 to 10 images per day. He discussed his working procedures in some detail in a series of articles for *Camera Craft,* reprinted in *Edward Weston on Photography,* 88-96.

One major area of his work not included in the Huntington collection is the nude study. Sexual imagery is not entirely absent, however. In two tree studies with decidedly male and female torsos [Pl. 14] Weston demonstrates that the human form could appear in the most unexpected places.

The book which resulted from the Guggenheim years, *California and the West,* contained not only his photographs but a narrative description of his travels, written by Charis Wilson, who had originally urged Weston to apply for the grant. Dedicated to the Guggenheim Foundation and Henry Allen Moe, this popular book has been through numerous reprintings and two editions. Its success seems to have provided later Guggenheim photographers with a prototype for their own publications. In a letter to his editor, Tom Maloney at U.S. Camera, the publishers of this work, Weston assessed the special importance of the Guggenheim photographs in his career:

With the exception of portraits and nudes, my Guggenheim period is a summation of my life-work; it includes every possible approach to seeing that I have touched before in a mature and conclusive form.[7]

7 Letter from Weston to Tom Maloney, September 1939, included in Charis Wilson's unpublished notes from the Guggenheim trip (hereafter referred to as LCW/MSS).

Although publication of a book was part of Weston's original plans, his direct involvement with the Huntington seems to have stemmed from his efforts to extend the grant for an additional year in 1938. According to correspondence between Moe and Weston,[8] it was Merle Armitage, the Los Angeles graphic designer and publisher, who first proposed that Weston produce a set of his Guggenheim prints for the Huntington Library. Well known for its rare book collection and particular interest in California history, the Huntington's prestige lent a certain credibility to Weston's decidedly more documentary aims in his Guggenheim project. Weston was thrilled with the prospect of the gift: "I am of course equally excited about the Huntington Library Collection. If this and a book come out of my fellowship I can almost consider it a life's work."[9]

8 Letter from Moe to Weston, 11/14/38, Scrapbook B. See also letters between Moe and Weston about the Huntington gift, dated from October 1938 through March 1939, in the Guggenheim files.

9 Letter to Moe, 10/8/38, Guggenheim files.

While his extensive travels in 1937 took him to remote desert and mountain regions, Weston also wanted to include western cities and towns in his Guggenheim project. Moreover he needed additional time to print his extensive backlog of negatives.[10] Late in 1938 Weston agreed to print a set of photographs for the Huntington. Although he initially indicated that he wanted to include a thousand prints in the set, Weston and Moe finally agreed that five hundred was a more realistic number.[11] Between 1940 and 1944, the prints were sent to the Huntington in batches of about one hundred each.

10 Between 1937 and 1938, Weston exposed approximately 1500 negatives. After the first eight months of his grant he had printed 721 of them. The Huntington's collection was printed separately between 1940 and 1944.

11 Letter from Moe to Weston, 7/21/39, in the Guggenheim files.

Plate 12.
Sandstone Concretion, Salton Sea, 1937
The Henry E. Huntington
Library and Art Gallery.

43

Plate 13.
Tomales Bay, North Coast, 1937
The Henry E. Huntington
Library and Art Gallery.

Because the printing time was so drawn out, Weston had the opportunity to add to the Guggenheim series photographs from his new work for the Limited Editions Club's publication of *Leaves of Grass*. This series included a greater number of urban and industrial views than did the Guggenheim work [Pl. 15]. Because Weston drew his subjects from the entire country, not just the West, and in response to the breadth of Whitman's poetic imagery, the *Leaves of Grass* series presents a more complex vision of American life. Weston's photographs are not to be construed however as illustrations of specific passages in Whitman's poems, a fact that Weston himself made quite clear.[12] His photographs of both rural and urban America for *Leaves of Grass* take up many of the themes that he explored in the Guggenheim project. The generative forces of nature, scenes of cemeteries and graves, and his love of folk art and architecture are present in this series as well. Whitman's text and Weston's photographs stand as complementary yet independent interpretations of American life.

12 See Richard Ehrlich's discussion of this point in his introduction to *Edward Weston, Leaves of Grass* (reprint of 1942 ed., New York, 1970).

Forty-nine photographs were finally selected for the book and only a few of these are represented among the group of ninety from this series which Weston deposited at the Huntington. The portrait of Mr. and Mrs. Fry of Burnet, Texas, is the only one in the current exhibition [Fig. 33]. Weston took over four hundred negatives for the *Leaves of Grass* project and printed at least a hundred and forty. As a result, any discussion of the relationship between text and image with regard to this project must take into account these unpublished photographs as well.[13]

Fig. 33.
*Mr. and Mrs. Fry
of Burnet, Texas*, 1941
The Henry E. Huntington
Library and Art Gallery

13 Letter to Moe, 9/26/41, in Guggenheim files. For a recent discussion of this publication see Alan Trachtenberg's essay "Edward Weston's America: The *Leaves of Grass* Project." in *E.W., Centennial Essays in Honor of Edward Weston* (Carmel, 1986).

Weston's concern with the integration of text and photographs in his publications is paralleled in the work of contemporary FSA photographers. For the most part, however, these photographers are grouped together as documentary rather than art photographers. Their photographic publications parallel an important, though subsequently overlooked, aspect of Weston's work.

When Moe first wrote to Weston to notify him of the Guggenheim award, he referred to the project as "a series of photographic documents of the West." And although Weston objected to the phrase "photographic documents," an important aspect of the Huntington's initial interest in Weston's photography was linked to his ability to provide a "pictorial record" of California.[14] At the time of the Library's inception in the 1920s, the distinction between documentary and art photography was considered to be clear, and the Huntington was interested in collecting historical photographs rather than art photography. These distinctions gradually became less rigid during the following decade however. Walter

14 Letter to Moe, 4/24/37, in Guggenheim files.

Plate 14.
Lake Tenaya, 1937
The Henry E. Huntington
Library and Art Gallery.

Arensberg, the prominent collector of modernist art and an admirer of Weston's more abstracted imagery, wrote to recommend his work to the Guggenheim, "both from the point of view of documentation of the American scene and from the point of view of technical excellence and creative imagination."[15]

15 Letter from Arensberg to Weston, 12/30/37, Scrapbook B.

Arensberg's use of the phrase "American scene" is interesting in this context because it links Weston's work with that of the social-realist painters of the 1930s. The phrase reoccurs in another letter of recommendation to the Guggenheim written by Rockwell Kent, an artist well known for his left-wing political stance during this period:

Your reputation as an artist in photography is such that you'd hardly need the endorsement of any one in coming before the Guggenheim Jury. I shall, however, be glad to endorse you as I believe that your American photographs would constitute a valuable record of the American scene.[16]

16 Letter from Kent to Weston, 10/14/36, in Scrapbook B.

The Guggenheim grant process itself brought Weston into closer contact with both documentary photographers and realist painters active in the thirties. When Weston was putting together his grant application he sent a copy to the noted FSA photographer, Dorothea Lange, and her husband, Paul Taylor, an economist at the University of California at Berkeley. At their suggestion he revised his original single paragraph proposal (quoted at the beginning) and submitted a more detailed, five-page essay which discussed at length his approach to photography. In addition he sent along a small pamphlet on photography which he had written for a series called "Know Your Museum."[17]

17 Edward Weston, *Photography* (Pasadena, 1934), reprinted in *Edward Weston on Photography*, 72-77.

Lange and Taylor were the first to notify Weston unofficially that he had received his grant. They probably received word through Dr. Carl Sauer, a close friend and professor of geography at Berkeley, who was on the Guggenheim selection committee. Lange later introduced Weston to Sauer when the photographer was seeking the extension of his grant for another year. In October of 1937, Weston and Sauer met in Berkeley and spent an evening drinking tequila and reminiscing about their travels in Mexico. Sauer even suggested some sites along the north coast of California that Weston might photograph. Writing to Lange about that evening, Weston referred to it as "a turning point in my life."[18] Lange too was impressed with the itinerary of Weston's photographing trips and expressed interest in joining him.[19] While Lange did not in fact accompany Weston on any of his trips, she and her husband later discussed his work with him as he printed the negatives.

18 Undated letter to Lange in Guggenheim files. Lange forwarded this letter to Moe with a note: "I send this to you because (knowing Edward) I fear that his more formal application for extension might not state his problem nearly so well."

19 CW/MSS, 2/22/38.

Another noted documentary photographer, Willard Van Dyke, did join Weston and Wilson

Fig. 34.
Judge Walker's Gallery, Elk, 1939
The Henry E. Huntington
Library and Art Gallery

on a trip through northern California. Van Dyke, like Weston, was a member of the Group *f*/64, an informal association of photographers who advocated "straight" photography and abhorred the manipulation of the photographic negative.[20] During this trip Weston and Charis Wilson were married on April 24, 1939 in the small coastal town of Elk. The ceremony was performed by a retired tintype photographer and judge, whose portrait studio Weston recorded [Fig. 34]. Since the Guggenheim grant had allowed Weston to give up his commercial portrait business and devote himself to his own work, this picture of an abandoned church and studio is particularly meaningful: it was not only a record of his marriage but a reminder of the economic exigencies of his former profession as a studio photographer. The image, included in *California and the West,* is close in style to the work of many of the documentary photographers of the period, including Van Dyke.

In 1936 the Guggenheim Foundation showed a strong preference for realism both in its selection of committee members and in its awards. Artists on the committee were Gifford Beal, James Earle Fraser, and Eugene Speicher, all of whose works were figurative rather than abstract. Furthermore, the artists who received grants that year were noted for their various realist styles. Aaron Bohrod, William Gropper, Joe Jones, George Grosz, and Frederico Le Brun had all, at some point in their careers, responded to social and political concerns. In retrospect, it seems rather odd that Weston's more overtly formalist approach should appeal to the selection committee. They may have perceived Weston's turn to "straight" photography as a rejection of the artifice so common in Pictorialist photography. Or, more importantly, they may have felt that his proposal to record the Western landscape and its people fitted the documentary mode currently practiced by the FSA photographers.

While Weston's work has often been praised for its abstract quality, the photographer himself acknowledged that his inspiration came directly from the real world, from nature:

No painter or sculptor can be wholly abstract. We cannot imagine forms not already existing in nature,—we know nothing else. Take the extreme abstractions of Brancusi: they are all based upon natural forms. I have often been accused of imitating his work,—and I most assuredly admire, and may have been "inspired" by it—which really means I have the same kind of (inner) eye, otherwise Rodin or Paul Manship might have influenced me. Actually, I have proved, through photography, that Nature has all the "abstract" (simplified) forms, Brancusi or any other artist can imagine. With my camera I go directly to Brancusi's source. I find ready to use, select, and isolate, what he has to "create."[21]

20 They met at Adams' studio in Oakland to review each others' work and present public exhibitions. Van Dyke arranged for Lange's work to be exhibited there as well. See Jean Tucker's introduction to the exhibition catalogue, *Group f/64* (St. Louis, 1978), 3-5.

21 Letter from Weston to Ansel Adams, 1/28/32, in Scrapbook B, also quoted by Nancy Newhall in *Edward Weston, The Flame of Recognition* (Millerton, N.Y., 1971), 44.

Plate 16.
Moonstone Beach, 1937
The Henry E. Huntington
Library and Art Gallery.

In an image such as *Sandstone Concretion* [Pl. 12], the formal parallels between Weston's work and that of modernists like Brancusi and Arp are immediately apparent. The rounded shapes of the sandstone, vertical orientation of the picture's format, and contrast of the darker form of the "figure" against the lighter background, all suggest however that this rock formation can be read as a human figure, a piece of natural, rather than man-made, sculpture. Weston's camera lens seems to have found a Brancusi in the middle of the desert. Thus an interesting, inanimate rock formation is given even fuller meaning in Weston's photograph: it is not merely an anthropomorphic shape, but one that is made richer by its associations with both an ancient geological world and the world of modern art.

Although he consciously avoided photographing people for the Guggenheim project, Weston stated that their presence was not altogether lacking in his imagery. He indicated that his landscapes represented more than just the features of the terrain:

It seems to me utterly naive that landscape—not that of the pictorial school—is not considered of "social significance" when it has far more important bearing on the human race of a given locale than excrescences called cities. By landscape, I mean every physical aspect of a region—weather, soil, wildflowers, mountain peaks—and its effect on the psyche and the physical appearance of the people.[22]

22 Correspondence between Weston and Ansel Adams, 12/3/34, Scrapbook B. Also in Nancy Newhall, 62.

In photographs of wrecked cars, deserted cabins, ghost towns, and discarded clothes, he sought to evoke the human element in the landscape.[23] And it is precisely in this type of imagery that Weston's work comes closest to realist painters and documentary photographers of the period.

23 Edward Weston, "My Photographs of California" in *Edward Weston on Photography*, 82.

A surrealist element in Weston's still-life compositions also ties his photography to the art of the 1930s. In a photograph of a worn out shoe and empty can of beans [Pl. 16], Weston presents his still-life subjects as if they were surrealist "found objects." They are "readymades," waiting to be found by his camera. Like the sandstone concretions, the formal organization of the scene is revealed by the photographic process. The carefully controlled lighting and framing of the lens emphasize the three-dimensionality and textures of the objects. Translucent bits of glass contrast markedly with the surface textures of cloth and paper. The highlighted, parallel blades of grass echo the shape of the shoe, and the uppermost piece of grass extends the rounded edge of the can in a sweeping arc across the composition.

Fig. 35.
Oregon Coast, 1939
The Henry E. Huntington
Library and Art Gallery

Fig. 36.
Death Valley, 1939
The Henry E. Huntington
Library and Art Gallery

Fig. 37.
Barn with Hex Signs,
Berks County, Pennsylvania, 1941
The Henry E. Huntington
Library and Art Gallery

Yet for all of its formal appeal, this photograph conveys readable meaning as well. There is something odd, slightly satirical, in the juxtaposition of a once-stylish shoe with the homier refuse of a can of beans. The worn instep and broken heel suggest age and even decay. The upside-down can and shards of glass are the discarded remnants of our consumer age. The modern viewer in addition recognizes immediately that the style of the shoe and label on the can date from another era, further compounding the sense that this image is about the past.

For the most part the Guggenheim series is comprised of landscapes or detailed studies of plant and rock forms. But even in the most abstract of these, his cloud pictures, it is possible to find coherent meaning. Weston's fascination with cloud patterns began with his Mexican work in the 1920s and continues unabated here. From the oceanside [Fig. 35] to the mountains [Pl. 17] and the desert [Fig. 36], he captured varying effects of light and dramatic shapes of clouds. The cloud studies represent Weston's most accomplished efforts to record fleeting, ephemeral form. Like the still-life studies of old shoes or the details of aging buildings, they too suggest the passage of time.

Many of the themes that scholars and the public alike have discerned in Weston's work are also present in the photographs of FSA photographers as well: the dominance of rural imagery; landscapes which focus on the evidence of man's work in plowed fields, fences [Pl. 13], and roadways; the love of humble, vernacular architecture and folk art [Fig. 37]. Above all, the theme of decline and death which permeates many Depression-age photographs, in scenes of graveyards [Pl. 18], abandoned automobiles and buildings, also persists in Weston's work from this period.

Admittedly, the FSA photographers were given a programmatic task by the government, to photograph the social effects of the Depression in rural America, to document hardship, dislocation, and despair. Weston's concerns were more the outgrowth of inner, aesthetic motives. In his cross-country rambles by car Weston sought out many of the same sights recorded by the FSA photographers: the agricultural fields of California, Louisiana plantations, and deserted small towns all across America. Weston's photographs of empty roads, highway signs, and old cars are images that emphasize the vagabond way of life experienced by many Americans during the 1930s. And Charis Wilson's much praised text in *California and the West* is a detailed travelogue which renders a vivid picture of their own privations, the meager rations and primitive camping gear that they took along on their Guggenheim trips.

Plate 17.
Lake Ediza, High Sierra, 1937
The Henry E. Huntington
Library and Art Gallery.

Plate 18.
Bonaventure Cemetery,
Savannah, Georgia, 1941
The Henry E. Huntington
Library and Art Gallery.

Fig. 38.
Dead Pelican, 1942
The Henry E. Huntington
Library and Art Gallery

Fig. 39.
Crescent Beach, North Coast, 1939
The Henry E. Huntington
Library and Art Gallery

Fig. 40.
Dead Man, Colorado Desert, 1937
The Henry E. Huntington
Library and Art Gallery

25 For a discussion of
this type of pub-
lication see John
Rogers Puckett,
*Five Photo-Textual
Documentaries from
the Great Depres-
sion* (Ann Arbor,
1981).

A sense of abandonment and death is particularly evident in the Guggenheim series. Images of dead animals and birds [Fig. 38], junked cars [Fig. 39], and crumbling buildings [Pl. 19] are intermingled with austere or sometimes lyrical landscapes. Most often these rather morbid subjects are isolated from the landscape or seen in close-up studies. One of the most startling images in this group is Weston's photograph of a dead man [Fig. 40]. Driving across the Colorado Desert in Southern California, on one of his early Guggenheim trips, Weston and Wilson came across a small sign asking assistance for a sick man. By the time they had reached the spot to which they were directed, the man was dead. Weston could not resist a photograph of his gaunt face and bristled hair. Charis Wilson's log notes that the few personal effects by the side of the body included a hobo's bundle with a tin cup and the address of relatives in Tennessee. They speculated that he hitch-hiked or rode the rails out West, but unfamiliar with the dangers posed by the desert had died of heat stroke.[24] Aside from a photograph of Charis Wilson, this tragic image is the only other portrait study published in *California and the West*.

24 See notes for
5/17/37 in CW/
MSS. Weston also
sent Moe a news-
paper clipping
reporting his dis-
covery of the body.

In the *Leaves of Grass* series, however, Weston portrays the human element in a more obvious and positive manner. Here, there are straightforward and kindly portraits of the common man set alongside scenes of the accomplishments of modern industry and architecture—trainyards, refineries, hydroelectric dams, and skyscrapers. The rural landscape is presented as well, but in a quieter and gentler mood than in the Guggenheim photographs. *Leaves of Grass* constitutes Weston's most humanistic body of work.

The two major publications of Weston's work during this period, *California and the West* and *Leaves of Grass,* are representative of a type of publication that has become increasingly popular over the past fifty years, the photographically illustrated documentary.[25] One of the first of these publications to appear in the Depression years was Erskine Caldwell and Margaret Bourke-White's *Have You Seen Their Faces,* published in 1937. A photographic essay on rural life in the south, the book is critical of racial prejudices, the impoverishment of the soil because of an overdependence on cotton, and the tenant-farming system. Among the photographs by Bourke-White, portraits dominate, but there are also scenes of empty fields, aging plantations, and wrecked cars, subjects similar to those found in Weston's work.

Perhaps the most important photographic publications of this type to precede Weston's books were those illustrated with Walker Evans' work. At the time Weston and Moe were engaged in detailed discussions about the publication of his Guggenheim photographs, there was a major exhibition of Evans' work at the Museum of Modern Art. Weston, particularly,

26 Letter from Weston to Moe, 10/8/38, Guggenheim files.

27 Letter from Weston to Moe, 4/14/40, Guggenheim files. Like Weston, Evans received an extension of the grant for an additional year in 1941 and second grant in 1959.

28 Walker Evans, *American Photographs* (The Museum of Modern Art: New York, 1938), 193.

29 Wright Morris, *Structures and Artifacts, Photographs, 1933-1954* (Sheldon Memorial Art Gallery, University of Nebraska, Lincoln), 4.

was interested to see what kind of book the Museum of Modern Art would produce.[26] *American Photographs,* published in 1938, was illustrated with Evans' photographs taken while working for the FSA in 1935 and 1936. When Evans later received a Guggenheim grant in 1940, Weston wrote to the Foundation to voice his approval, calling Evans one of America's best photographers.[27]

In an essay in *American Photographs,* the critic Lincoln Kirsten wrote a description of Evans' photographs that might apply to Weston's just as well:

In intention and in effect they exist as a collection of statements deriving from and presenting a consistent attitude. Looked at in sequence they are overwhelming in their exhaustiveness of detail, their poetry of contrast, and, for those who wish to see it, their moral implication.[28]

Since its first grant to Weston, the Guggenheim Foundation has given substantial support to photographers interested in documenting various aspects of American life. In 1940 Dorothea Lange and Paul Taylor published their most important work of the Depression years, *An American Exodus,* and the following year Lange received a Guggenheim grant. Wright Morris, a Guggenheim recipient in 1942 and 1946, was another documentary photographer who dedicated his books to the Foundation and Henry Moe. Morris' *The Inhabitants* (1946) and *The Home Place* (1948), books dealing with the plight of rural Americans, are illustrated with images of vernacular architecture and the landscape but contain few scenes with people. Like Weston, Morris preferred to rely on single objects or buildings to convey their presence:

It is my feeling that the absence of people in these photographs enhances their presence as the objects—the structures, the artifacts, even the landscape suggest its appropriate inhabitant.[29]

Other recipients of Guggenheim grants for photography include Roy De Carava (1952), the first black photographer to receive a Guggenheim; Jack Delano (1945), another FSA-trained photographer; Helen Levitt (1959 and 1960), well-known for her urban scenes; and Robert Frank (1955 and 1960), the first European-born photographer to be awarded a grant. Frank's Guggenheim photographs were published in a book called *The Americans,* with an introduction by Jack Kerouac, yet another inveterate traveler and poet of America's highways.

The photographs in these books, Weston's included, are invaluable cultural records. In each case however, the artistry of the individual photographer transforms the documentary mode

Plate 19.
Harmony Borax Works,
Death Valley, 1938
The Henry E. Huntington
Library and Art Gallery.

Plate 20.
Death Valley, 1938
The Henry E. Huntington
Library and Art Gallery.

from mere factual reportage to subjective interpretation. In the process of elevating the status of these photographs to art, exhibitions and publications often lessen their social impact. In a letter to Ansel Adams (another Guggenheim recipient in 1946, 1948, and 1959), Edward Weston wrote of the complex interplay between the documentary and artistic modes that existed during this period:

I agree with you that there is just as much "social significance in a rock" as "in a line of unemployed." All depends on the seeing. *I must do the work I am best suited for...we* [documentary and art photographers] *all have our place, and should function together as a great fugue. And the tensions between opposites is necessary.*[30]

30 Letter from Weston to Ansel Adams, 12/3/34 in the Archives of the Center for Creative Photography.

Weston's photographs in the Huntington collection reveal those tensions more than any other body of his work. Tensions exist in the contrast between images about life and death, male and female, the natural and the man-made, in a patch of seaweed and the endless expanse of sand dune.

Weston's photographs have been seen as standing apart from the documentary photographic movement of the 1930s and 40s, but close study of his work in the Huntington collection reveals that he shared many of the same concerns and working methods, if not ultimately the political stance of some of his contemporaries. Although he often photographed farmers and rural artisans who suffered great hardship during the Depression years, Weston maintained what he felt was an essentially apolitical attitude toward their plight. His own meager subsistence during these years however provided a common bond with their precarious economic situtation. The enduring appeal of Weston's art lies in his ability to suggest, rather than state overtly, the humanist values associated with his subjects.

Susan Danly

The 50 works in the Huntington exhibition are drawn from a collection of over 500 prints. Weston's original gift included a selection of approximately 30 photographs from the 1920s and early 1930s; 250 photographs made on his Guggenheim grant between 1937 and 1939; 90 photographs shot on his travels from New England through the South and Southwest in the early 1940s; 100 photographs of Point Lobos and Carmel taken in the 1930s and 40s; and 16 photographs of the dunes at Oceano, California from 1936. Over the years the Huntington Library has also added several examples of Weston's early Los Angeles work from his father's archery notebooks and a selection of his commercial portrait photographs.

All of Weston's photographs in the Huntington's Guggenheim collection are approximately 8 x 10 inch contact prints mounted on board. They are titled, signed, and dated in pencil by Weston on the verso of the mount. Weston also included his negative numbers on these prints. They are identified below by accession number.

1	*Shell.* 1927. 000.111.494
2	*White Radish.* 1933. 000.111.492
3	*Dry Kelp, Point Lobos.* 1934. 000.111.206
4	*Dunes, Oceano.* 1936. 000.111.262
5	*Moonstone Beach.* 1937. 000.111.353
6	*Little River, North Coast.* 1937. 000.111.158
7	*Modoc Lava Beds, California.* 1937. 000.111.144
8	*Child's Grave, Marin County.* 1937. 000.111.170
9	*Tomales, North Coast.* 1937. 000.111.172
10	*Cabin, High Sierra Nevada.* 1937. 000.111.280
11	*Tenaya Lake, High Sierra Nevada.* 1937. 000.111.286

48 *Frank Lloyd Wright's Taliesin West, Phoenix, Arizona.* 1941. 000.111.102

49 *Dead Pelican, Point Lobos.* 1942. 000.111.237

50 *Kitty John on Lili's Stump.* 1944. 000.111.477

Designed by James Marrin, Pasadena, California.

Typography set in Garamond Number 3 by Phototype House, Los Angeles, California.

Printed in an edition of 3,000 by Gardner/Fulmer Lithograph, Buena Park, California.

Copy photography for the Huntington Library collection by Robert Schlosser.

Copy photography for the J. Paul Getty Museum collection by Stephenie Blakemore.